Workplace Race

**Get promoted first.
Survive the downsizing.
Be the employee you'll want
     when you're the boss.**

J. Adam Myrna
and
John W. Myrna

The Short Attention Span Library
Quick Study Press
Alexandria, Virginia

This book is available at a discount when ordered in bulk. For information contact the publisher.

Quick Study Press
3826 Jay Avenue
Alexandria, VA 22302
(703) 931-3620
quickstudy@aol.com

Copyright© 1998, by John W. Myrna.
All rights reserved. No part of this publication may be stored in a retrieval system or copied in any way without permission from the publisher.

ISBN 1-891660-02-0

Cover design by Hanlon Dorsey Advertising.
Printed in the United States of America.

Acknowledgements

Adam and John would like to thank the many people who helped put this book together, in particular Janet Horgen, Anne Bullard, Jennifer Gans, and Kathern Myrna for their careful editing and many suggestions.

Introduction

There's no introduction.
You're in a hurry

A task "almost finished" is valueless. Divide tasks into several useful parts that can be completed one by one in a timely manner.

Be open to new information and insights. Remember that every good invention was once ridiculed. ("What do we need electric light for? My oil lamp works just fine!")

Compliment people when they do a good job—be specific. A compliment about a specific piece of work carries more weight than a general "you're doing good."

Always deliver on every commitment, no matter what personal price you have to pay. Make few commitments, but always deliver.

Keep a business card handy or pen with the company name on it for people to use. Keeping the company name in the minds of potential customers helps the company succeed, and its success helps you, too.

Overestimate what your projects require. Think of Scotty from the "Star Trek" series. He always gave himself some breathing room to account for the unknowns and to make himself a hero.

Always summarize a new project and write down the expected results before starting. Get your manager to review your summary to assess and acknowledge your understanding of the project *before* starting.

Appearances are as important as the actual fact. People believe what they see. They'll think you're a shirker if you show up late for work this morning—even if you worked late last night. Sometimes life can be unfair.

Ask someone you trust about your unfavorable qualities. Take what you hear to heart and change things accordingly.

Attend your company picnics and holiday parties. Attendance demonstrates support for the company, allows people to see you in a different light . . . and could be fun.

Avoid making people who are infrequent users of a system feel stupid by overwhelming them with incomprehensible jargon and detail.

Be aware of your behavior. The reality is that you become what you do. The positive behavior you exhibit today is the behavior people will expect—and reward—in the future.

Be careful using freight elevators—don't ask!

Build a personal intelligence network. Be friends with the people who know what's really going on.

By all means help people, but first determine how much they already know. Avoid talking down to people. They may already know the general facts and only need help in a very specific area.

Choose the right company or organization for you to work for. When you walk in the door do you feel a negative tension or a sense of excitement? Does everyone rush out at closing time or does the work environment feed people's passion?

Clarify everybody's expectations before you start a task. The quality of your work is the only real measure of your worth, and quality consists of meeting or exceeding expectations.

Contribute at least one idea at every staff meeting. Work to become part of the solution.

Decorate your desk for the holiday season: it brightens everyone's day.

Demand a comfortable chair and wear comfortable shoes. Buy the chair yourself if you have to. When you're not comfortable, you can't perform your best.

Demonstrate that you have a vested interest in your company's success. For example, purchase stock in the company.

Do something specific each week to make work easier for you and your co-workers. Management gurus call it continuous improvement. Remember to keep track of these improvements for your annual performance review.

Do things that support people, make friends, and keep you in the loop. Keep a bottle of aspirin in your desk for co-workers and yourself. Keep a dish of candy on your desk. Post positive, humorous cartoons or memorable quotes near your desk.

Don't automatically believe office gossip. Talk directly to your managers and co-workers and make your own determinations.

Don't be afraid to change your mind when you receive new information or gain new insight.

Don't be afraid to invest in yourself. If your company doesn't have a program to pay for books, tools or training then invest your own money. You will be rewarded with a higher salary when you become more skilled, productive, and valuable—even if you have to move to a different department or company to realize the reward.

Don't be afraid to say no to a position offered to you that you can't handle. Carefully explain your reasoning, thank them for asking, and suggest someone else you think is ready to handle it.

Don't be afraid to talk to your manager or your manager's manager. Follow company protocol but never allow fear to prevent the people who can act on your good ideas from hearing them.

Don't hold back because you're worried your manager won't notice your achievements. Perform your best, and people *will* take notice.

Don't risk injuring yourself trying to lift 100-pound objects. Always ask for help.

Don't spread rumors.

Don't take the extra time to back into a parking space in the morning—it sends a clear signal that leaving quickly at the end of the day is more important to you than getting started on time.

Don't use big words simply for the sake of using them. It obfuscates meaning and makes you sound pedantic. State things as simply and concisely as possible while still being professional. Don't make people feel stupid when they talk to you.

Don't waste time making excuses. Own up to a problem, explain what you will do to fix it, and make sure it will never happen again.

Don't fret about not being paid for working extra hours as long as you are gaining experience and skills. Remember that you are first and foremost investing in your own career.

Don't worry about who gets credit for a good idea. What goes around comes around.

Find out what the vision and mission of your company is. Ask yourself: What am I doing that contributes to the achievement of those goals?

Focus on defining problems rather than placing blame. Placing blame antagonizes people and keeps the focus on the past.

Force yourself to learn and use a new feature of your software with every new project.

Fuel your car on the way home from work. Running out of fuel in the morning is not a valid excuse to be late.

Get a telephone headset. Having two free hands while you talk on the phone can create a surprising increase in your productivity.

Have something that makes you memorable—a unique shirt, tie, scarf, handkerchief, expression, positive attitude, etc.

Remember the sea squirt.
It uses its simple brain to locate a safe rock to attach to and then it eats its brain.
Companies *do not* want sea squirts as employees.

Hold the door for other people.

If you don't ask, the answer is no.

If you don't know the answer, don't make one up. You'll be found out and then nothing you say will be completely believed.

If you can't sell someone on your good idea, build a prototype. It's hard for most people to embrace the intangible—make your idea tangible.

If you see a better way to do something, do it that way yourself and then share your successful approach with others.

If you see a better approach to do something than what your organization requires, consider doing it *both* ways and let others choose the winning approach.

If you see a piece of trash on the floor, pick it up and throw it away. This is your environment, your life and your company.

If you see something that will improve productivity, but your manager will not approve of the expenditure, consider funding it yourself.

If you want to hunt buffalo, dress like a buffalo. If you want to be a manager, dress like a manager.

If you're going to get yourself a soda or snack, ask if anyone else wants one and get it for them. Don't worry about being reimbursed; consider it an investment in generating good will.

If you've been sitting at your desk all day, get up and take a brief walk—it gives you a new perspective.

If you've run out of things to do, find someone who needs help.

In every disagreement, step back and *force* yourself to see and consider all sides.

It's impossible to be right all the time. Keep your humility. Remember that overconfidence easily becomes arrogance.

Remember that only you are responsible for your career. You are responsible for making sure you get quality reviews, receive fair compensation, and grow personally and professionally.

You're working at the right place if you are steadily increasing your market value, working with good people and being fairly compensated. If any one of these three is not true, it's up to you to change things.

Jot down your daily accomplishments. Just before your annual performance review assemble your notes into a memo. Give the memo to your manager before your review to highlight the good things that you've done during the past year that may have been forgotten.

When you stop learning, it's time for a new job.

Set your sights on your next position soon after you're promoted. Identify the gaps in your skills and experience and then put a personal development program in place to fill those gaps. Like magic, you will be ready when opportunity knocks in a couple of years.

Keep a tape recorder or paper on hand to document those flashes of insight.

Keep an open mind and be flexible in your opinions. Don't let yourself rush to judge.

Keep a razor or makeup in your car or desk for those mornings when you rush out the door and forget the basics.

Keep your car clean. You never know when your boss might need a lift.

Keep your desk organized rather than cleared. Empty desk—empty mind?

Keep your memos and e-mails short and to the point.

Learn how to do your manager's job.

Learn how to make coffee, clear copier jams, program the phone system, reset circuit breakers, and restart the network, and people will think you're a god.

Don't accept so many tasks that you can't deliver quality work. Keep a list of current projects and priorities. Whenever you're assigned to take on something new, ask yourself and your manager what on your list is less important and can be deferred. Make sure everyone understands the consequences of adding a new task.

Learn how to say no by sharing the other commitments and priorities you're operating under.

Learn how to touch-type. Even if it's not a requirement for your job, it increases your productivity and value.

Learn people's names. Even better, learn the names of your co-workers' spouses and children, and learn about their special events. People want to work with people who care about them.

When you first meet someone, smile, shake their hand and use their name.

Greet everyone you pass in the hall, by name.

Learn to anticipate the repercussions of your actions. Identify who will be affected by your actions and give them a timely "heads up."

Make a point of learning and fully utilizing new office systems such as the telephone system, computer, photocopier, fax, etc. Using specialized features that most people never bother to learn about can give you a significant productivity edge.

Often it is more effective to take action first and apologize later than to ask formal permission. Just be sure to identify potential consequences first, and stand ready to accept them.

Never call in sick on a Friday or Monday unless absolutely necessary. People who appear to get sick frequently on Fridays or Mondays raise a red flag.

Save sick days for when you are really sick. When you are really sick, take the sick leave. Don't bring your flu to the office to share. People won't appreciate it and your performance will be poor.

Don't lie. It's hard enough to keep the truth straight, and you will eventually forget to whom you told which lie.

Don't make enemies. Life is short enough, and enemies have a way of reappearing at critical points in your life or career.

Don't make fun of someone for asking simple questions or for help. You diminish yourself, you lose an opportunity to build good will, and you condition people to remain ignorant and unproductive. People avoid anyone that makes them feel stupid.

Don't point out problems without presenting solutions.

Don't say that you will *try* to get something done. Decide to do it or not do it. Life's too short to work with people who merely try.

Never take advantage of expense reports or travel allowances. Trust is the lubricant of success. If you can't be trusted with the small stuff, how can you be trusted with the big things?

Don't take credit for someone else's ideas. The truth always has a way of coming out.

No cheap shots.

No matter how frantic the work pace is with the need to work evenings and weekends, always take at least one full day a week for yourself.

No surprises. Never embarrass your boss or co-workers—even with good news.

Once you accept responsibility for part of a project, remember that you're not done until the entire project is finished. *You can't produce results unless you finish what you start!*

People become leaders when those being led consider them leaders. A title doesn't create a leader, it simply recognizes existing leadership. Act like a leader and you will become a leader.

Pick your battles. Carefully consider what is truly important to you. Don't sacrifice your good will fighting over small issues like parking spaces and free coffee.

Imagine you're the owner or manager and be the employee you wish you had hired.

Remember that it's great to help someone, but it doesn't help them in the long run if you always end up doing their job for them.

Remember that privacy is never guaranteed at the office. Imagine someone accidentally reading the memos, notes, messages, computer files, letters or e-mail you leave lying around.

Remember that it's the customer who pays your salary—the company just processes the check.

Remember that nothing happens until someone sells something. No matter what your position is, you are first and foremost a salesman.

Remember that if you are truly irreplaceable, you can't be promoted.

Respect your co-workers' privacy, but if you learn of a serious issue such as employee theft, inform your management at once.

Establish and vocalize expectations up front. Over the course of the project continue to remind everyone involved what the expected results are. Far too often projects are considered a failure for failing to meet someone's "secret expectations."

Start the day with a good breakfast—it will set the tone for your performance the entire day. If you're in too much of a hurry, keep a case in the car of one of the well-balanced liquid meals like Sweet Success® or Slim•Fast®.

Stay focused. If you lose sight of your goal, stop and regain it, no matter what it takes. Without focus you can't be productive.

Take prudent risks and accept the fact that not everything you try will work. Babe Ruth held the record for strikeouts as well as home runs.

Take responsibility for 100% of the communication between you and your manager and team. Ask people to paraphrase what you just said as a way to verify their comprehension.

Take vacations to recharge and regain perspective. The vacation must be long enough to make a difference. Try to schedule vacations to overlap a company holiday—you can leave Friday and return Monday 10 days later and be out of the office for only four full business days.

No one wants to work with someone who looks like they're in a hurry to leave. Take your jacket off, roll up your sleeves, and "stay a while."

The only way to get something done is to take action and do it. Talking, making lists, and setting goals are important steps, but they are meaningless until someone takes action.

The way you behave and function as an employee can give you the knowledge and abilities necessary to be a good employer.

There is a rule of factors of ten. 7 key chunks of specific knowledge will enable you to chitchat about any area of the business. Ten times that—70 chunks—will allow you to be minimally functional. With 700 you'll be fully functional, 7,000 an expert, and 70,000 a guru. The more you learn about your specific area, the more likely you will be recognized as an expert or guru. If you invest in learning 7-70 chunks of knowledge about several areas, you will be an exceptionally valuable resource for your company.

Think of your manager as your coach. Identify the help you need to be successful and ask your manager for coaching and counseling.

Ultimately, you're working for yourself. Investing more time and energy in avoiding work than doing it hurts you more than your employer.

Volunteer for special projects. Better yet, volunteer to head special projects. Special projects are a way to gain valuable new experience, add value to the company—and get noticed.

Volunteer to take the minutes during a staff meeting. In many ways the person who documents a meeting defines its outcome.

Volunteer to write for the company newsletter. You stand out for the effort and others, including your boss's boss, learn about you.

Watch your language and respect others' sensitivities to certain words. If your idea of swearing is different than your boss's or co-workers' you can easily offend them.

When estimating, remember the following rule of thumb: everyone thinks they can complete 10 times more than they have time to do. (Only 1 out of every 10 items on your to-do list will get finished.)

When giving instructions, always be specific about the *results* you expect. A vague description of your expectations usually results in a disappointing outcome. However, give others a chance to deliver high-quality creative work by not overwhelming them with too many details on *how* you want them to produce those results.

When interacting with people, focus on what they can do rather than what they can't do.

When you finish reading a good technical or business book, pass it on to someone else. You increase their skills, show you care about them and your company and you're remembered as the knowledgeable person.

When you see someone in need, don't hesitate to help them—but don't embarrass them in the process.

When you see something wrong, be the person who steps forward and offers a solution.

When you see two co-workers arguing, don't interfere. You don't want to end up in somebody's "camp."

Whenever you're hit with a big problem or project, take some time to gain perspective and prepare rather than rush in. Understanding the "big picture" always leads to a better result.

Why did the chicken cross the road? Never do a project unless you understand why it's being done. You can't do a project well unless you understand the expected results.

Work smarter, not harder? Work smarter *and* harder!

You don't need reserved parking if you are one of the first people to show up for work.

You're paid for results, not activity. Ask yourself what 3-5 key *results* your company depends on you to produce.

Your ability to learn on the job is more valuable than any skills you currently have.

What works for you?

Tell us your favorite tip for getting along with employers, co-workers, suppliers and customers.

Send your comments to:
johnw@myrna.com

About the authors...

Adam Myrna's entrepreneurial ideas first emerged at age nine when he started selling pencils at school for ten cents each and dreamed of one day running his own company. By the age of fourteen he had teamed up with a good friend to develop and market Apple II software. During the summer before college he tried to get a job in the traditional business world and was told his lack of real experience made him more of a liability than an asset. In response, Adam began a business venture buying and selling used equipment at computer shows. Success made him confident that he had what it took to be an entrepreneur.

In a series of part-time technical jobs while attending school, Adam drifted into poor work habits. Because of his specialized skills, he felt that he had earned the right to ease up a bit, surf the Internet at will, and deliver little more than the bare minimum his bosses required. His job performance when working for others was, needless to say, not even close to his potential or personal standards.

By 21 the entrepreneurial urge had grabbed Adam full force, and with a financial backer, he opened a retail storefront to sell and service personal computers. Becoming an employer for the first time proved to be a real eye-opener. He found the people working for him behaved the same way he had when he worked for others. He now had to live with the negative impact of these behaviors.

After folding the business, Adam faced a moment of truth. His attempts at running companies thus far were unsuccessful and Adam needed to figure out why. It appeared that drive and talent were not enough. He had to be able to find, manage, and motivate *quality* employees. So, in the interest of being a better employer in the future, Adam decided to become a great employee.

He soon took a job as a field technician. Starting the first day he set a personal daily goal to *be the employee he wished he could have hired*. This focus, supported by his talent, hard work, long hours, and dedication, soon caught the attention of his manager and other superiors. He was rapidly promoted while finding work a lot more enjoyable.

This book provides its readers with numerous tips on how to be a better employee – and ultimately a more successful one. Adam, however, is not finished. The skills and talents he refines while working and the insights he gains about employee needs and wants, are making him a better manager and future employer.

John Myrna is a recognized turnaround artist. Although he doesn't call it art. John calls it *planning*. After a career with a successful start-up, John's first turn-around was a company with cash only for two months' payroll and zero sales. Its board asked John to save the company and jobs. Within two years he had the company second in its market, attracting new capital and growing with sales and acquisitions.

July 4, 1991, John and Mary Myrna founded Myrna Associates Inc., dedicated to improving the competitiveness of America's small businesses through strategic planning. John's experiences have given him a passionate belief in the power of strategic planning to generate immediate bottom-line results during business transitions like growth spurts, financial crises, turnarounds and acquisitions. He's distilled his 20 years of experience leading companies out of trouble into a short, intense two-day strategic planning program tailored for small to medium-sized companies. It delivers more in two days than the two weeks required by traditional "big company" retreats. Even companies in crisis can find two days to invest.

John's Total Quality Planning™ (TQP) succeeds because of the executive team's consensus and commitment to a small number of goals. John facilitates the process and handles pre-planning, meeting arrangements, transcribing and printing the plan. The final plan is in hand within four working days.

The challenge of finding, motivating and retaining quality employees has been a topic nearly every week when John meets with executive teams across the country. When his son Adam started talking about the same topic, a collaborative book was the natural result.

For more information on strategic planning, contact John at Myrna Associates, Inc. (800) 207-8192, johnw@myrna.com, or check his web site at http://www.myrna.com.

Quick Study Press recognizes that in today's business environment many people are rushed, yet still need vital information. The Short Attention Span Library accommodates that need in a series of compact books that focus on short statements of facts, solutions or ideas that work. We leave discussions of history or psychology to the longer formats. These are books for people in a hurry.

Short Attention Span Library titles may be ordered in bulk at a discount. For further information contact:
Quick Study Press
3826 Jay Avenue
Alexandria, VA 22302
(703) 931-3620
E-mail: quickstudy@aol.com

The Short Attention Span Library series includes short, compact books on these topics:

- Strategic Planning
- Time Management
- Launching New Products
- Advertising
- Success
- Motivation
- Selling Skills

Upcoming topics:

- Accounting
- Coaching
- Investing
- Meetings
- Stress
- Presentation Skills
- Customer Service
- Success at Work
- Benchmarks
- Creativity

Other books by John W. Myrna

100 Quick Tips for Business Success
  Business tips for CEOs.

How to Implement Total Quality Planning™
  Breakthrough program to create a strategic long range plan in two days.